D●TS BY DONNA

The
Animal
Alphabet

abc

The Animal Alphabet

is for alpaca

Austin the alpaca is a cute, quirky member of the camel family from South America. Alpacas are very social and like to live in herds. Just don't get too close, or they might spit at you!

b
is for bear

Beryl the bear lives in a forest in the Northern Hemisphere. She is a brown bear, also known as a grizzly bear, and has long, thick fur. Bears sleep in dens and hibernate in winter.

C

is for cat

Catherine the cat is a beautiful pet. Cats sleep between 12 and 16 hours a day, and can be active at both day and night. Cats are very flexible and can land on their feet from great heights.

d

is for dog

Daphne the dog is an adorable pet. Dogs are very social and love to spend time with their families. They are easy to train, and some breeds can work as service dogs or guide dogs.

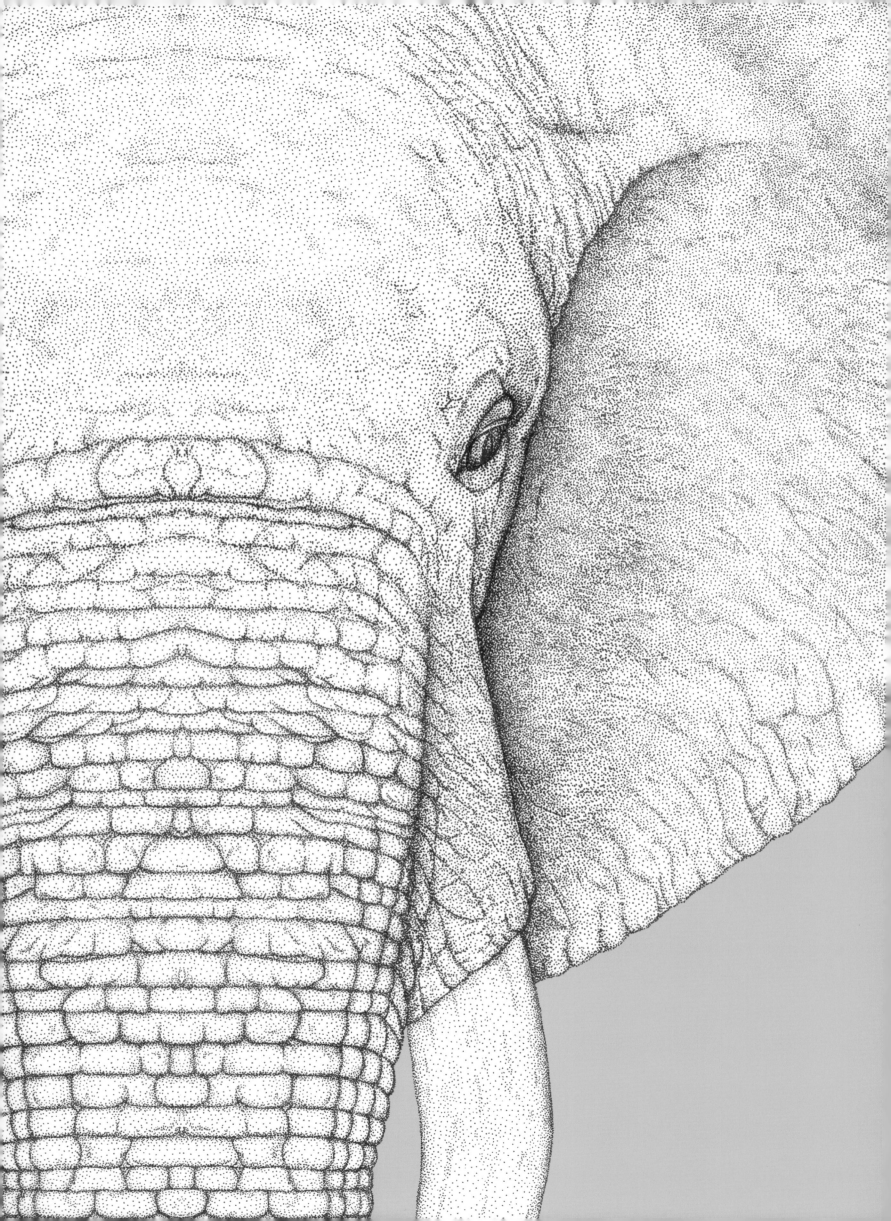

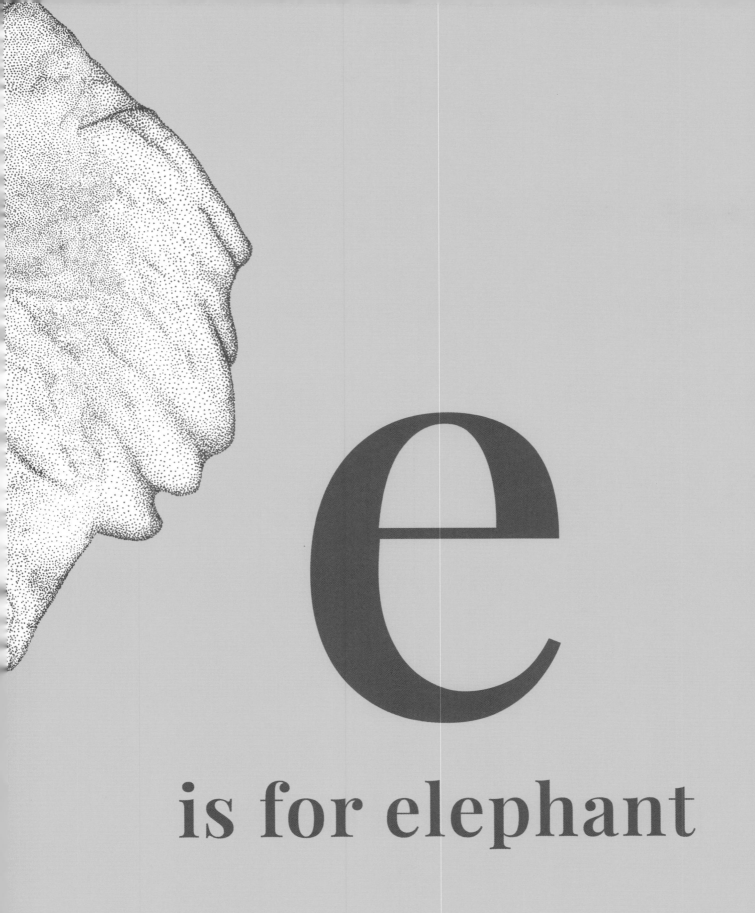

e
is for elephant

Ethan the elephant is the world's largest land animal. There are three species of elephant: African Savannah (Bush), African Forest and Asian. They can live to be up to 70 years old.

f

is for fox

Franklin the fox looks cute and cuddly, but he is a fierce hunter! Red foxes are mainly nocturnal, and can live in both urban and rural areas. They have pointy ears, bushy tails and reddish-brown fur.

g

is for giraffe

Georgi the giraffe is a herbivore, meaning she only eats plants. Giraffes' long necks and strong blue tongues help them reach the leaves in the treetops. A group of giraffes is called a 'tower'.

h

is for hippo

Harper the hippo spends most of her day in the rivers and lakes of Africa. Hippopotamuses can see and breathe while their bodies are under water, because their eyes, nose and ears are located on the top of their heads.

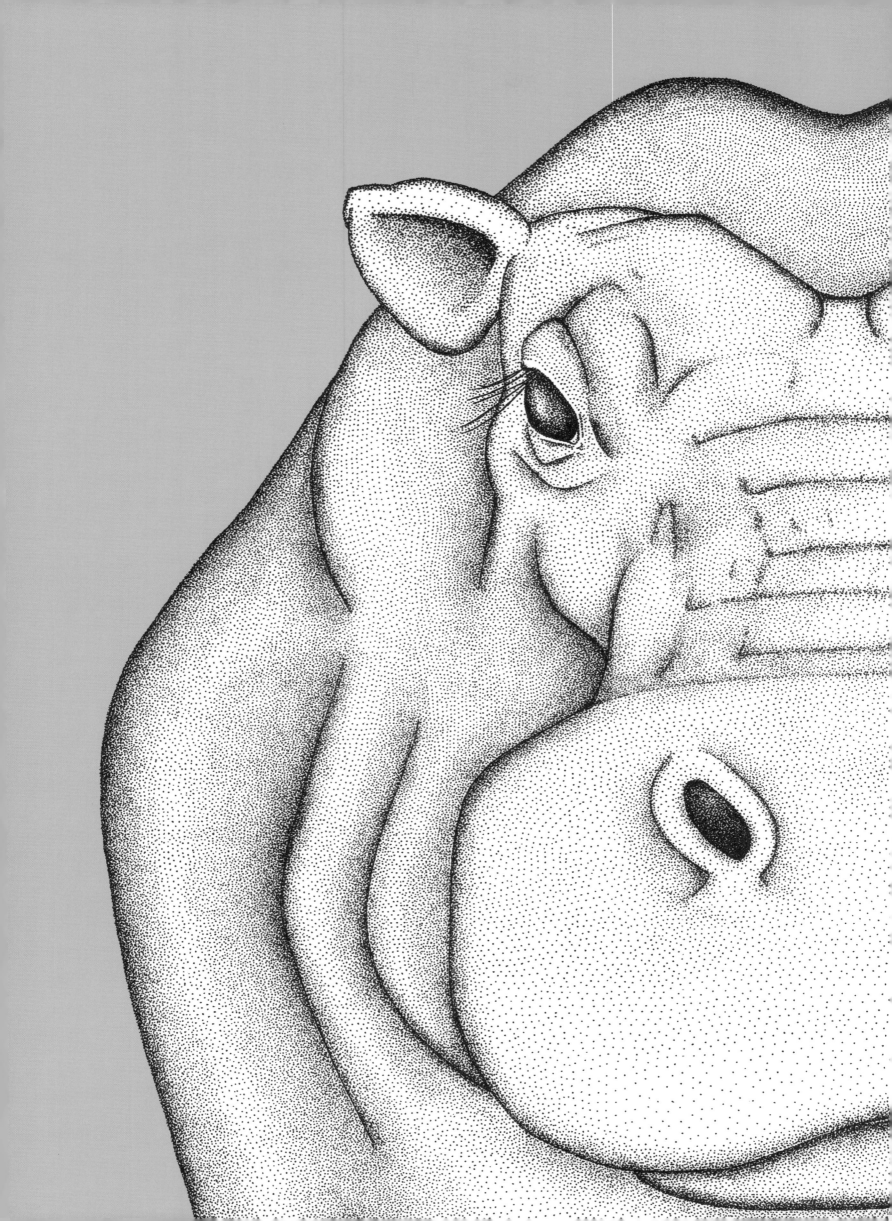

i

is for iguana

Indy the iguana prefers warm, tropical temperatures. Iguanas like to live in trees, and they can run fast and even swim. If an iguana loses its tail, it can grow another one in its place!

j

is for joey

Jasmine the joey is a baby kangaroo. Joeys stay in their mother's pouch for six months. Then they start making short trips out of the pouch, before becoming fully independent at 10 months old.

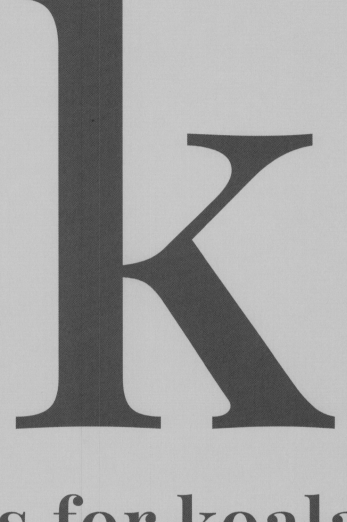

k

is for koala

Kerry the koala is an iconic Australian marsupial. Koalas live in eucalyptus trees, where they eat the leaves and spend most of the time sleeping – up to 20 hours a day!

l

is for lion

Leo the lion is the most majestic and courageous animal of all! Lions are the only big cats that live in a group, known as a 'pride'. Each lion has a unique and distinct roar.

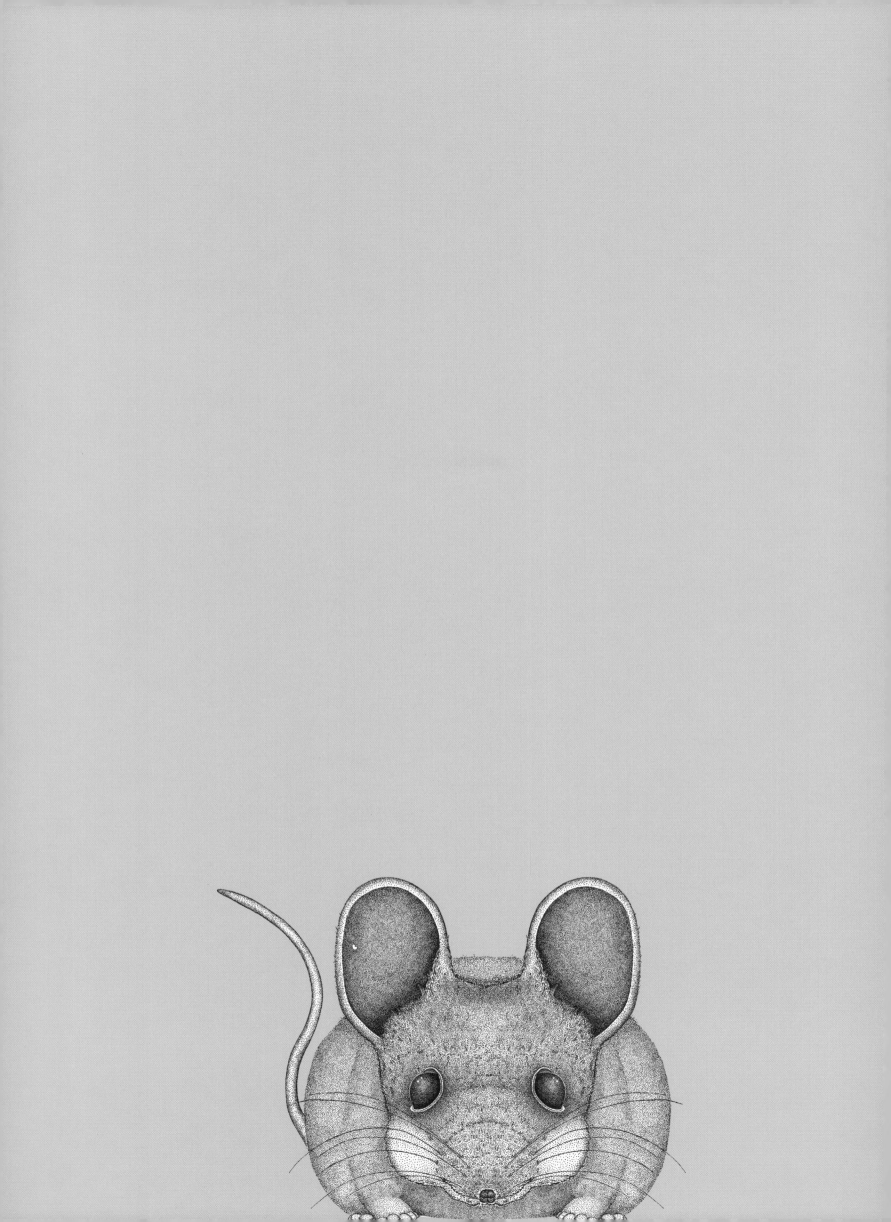

m

is for mouse

Milla the mouse is the most common rodent in the world. Mice can live outside but they prefer to live indoors. Their population can grow very fast – a female mouse can have up to 150 babies a year!

n

is for narwhal

Nahlah the narwhal is a whale with a large tusk on her head. Narwhals live in the icy waters of the Arctic Ocean, and are typically found in pods of up to 20 individuals.

is for orangutan

Ollie the orangutan is part of the great ape family. Orangutans live in tropical rainforests on the islands of Borneo and Sumatra in Asia. They are closely related to humans, sharing 97 per cent of our DNA!

p

is for panda

Pete the panda is a gorgeous bear that lives in mountain ranges in Asia. The panda diet consists mostly of bamboo, and they have a long wrist bone that they use like a thumb to grip their food.

q
is for queen bee

Quinn the queen bee is the mother of the hive. She can lay up to 2000 eggs a day. Bees are very important – as well as producing honey, they pollinate flowers, fruit and vegetables.

r

is for rhino

Reggie the rhino has two large horns on his head, which grow continuously during his lifetime. Rhinoceroses live in hot areas in Africa and Asia, and they often wallow in mud to keep cool.

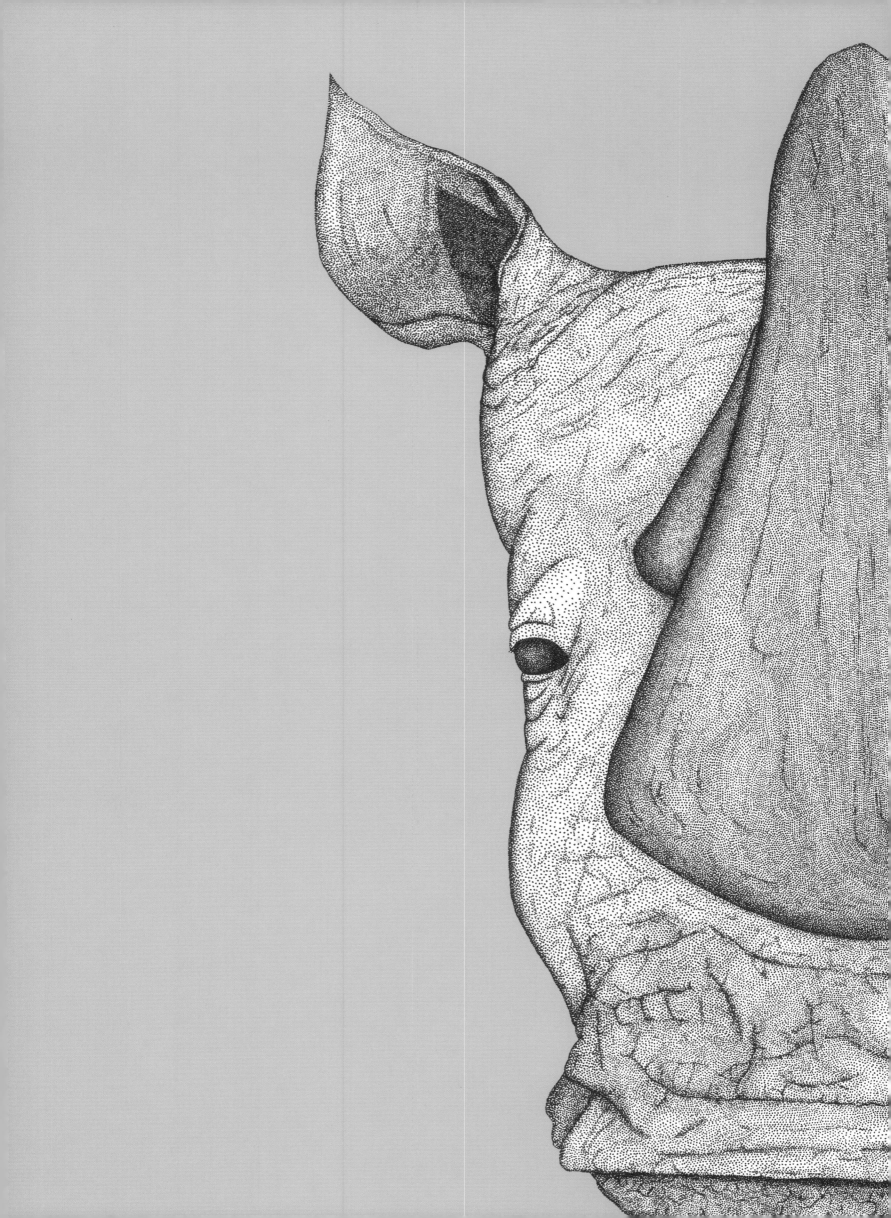

S

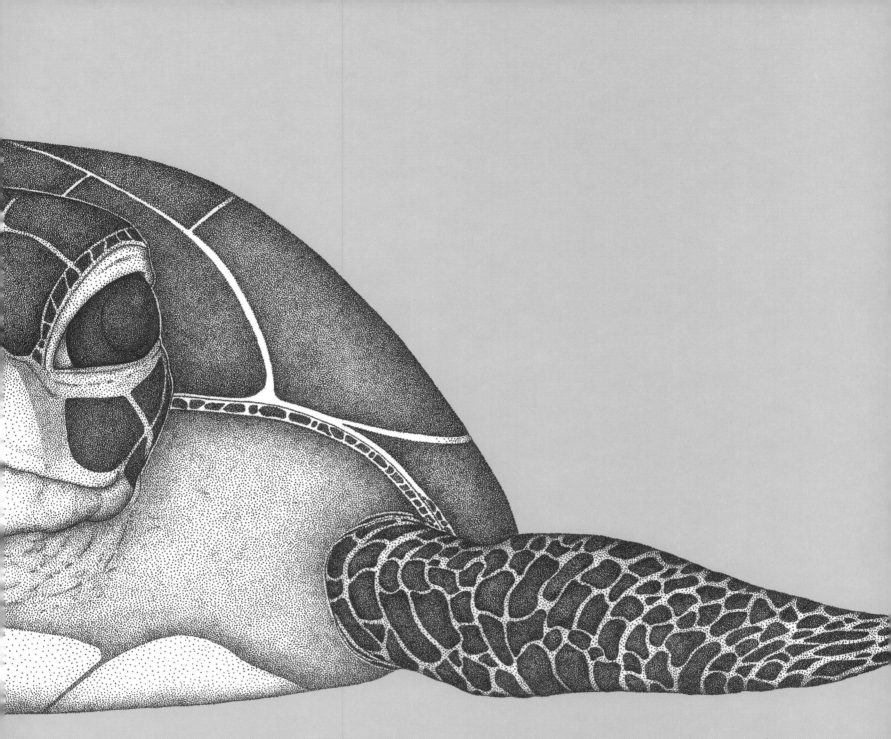

is for sea turtle

Susan the sea turtle has a hard shell on her back that protects her body. Sea turtles spend most of their lives swimming in the ocean, but females will come ashore to nest.

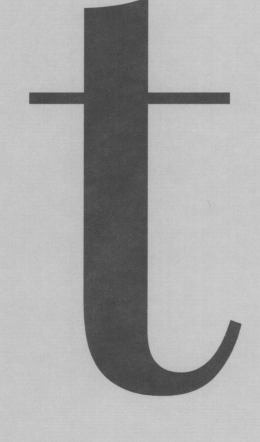

t
is for tiger

Timothy the tiger is the largest wild cat in the world! Tigers are native to Asia, and are solitary hunters that search for food alone at night. Each tiger's stripey pattern is unique.

U

is for ulysses butterfly

Una the ulysses butterfly is one of the most unique and distinctive butterfly species, with bright blue wings. Ulysses butterflies live in tropical rainforest areas such as north-eastern Australia and Papua New Guinea.

V

is for vampire bat

Victor the vampire bat feeds on animal blood!
Vampire bats are nocturnal animals that hunt at night.
They live in caves or dark areas in Mexico and Central
and South America.

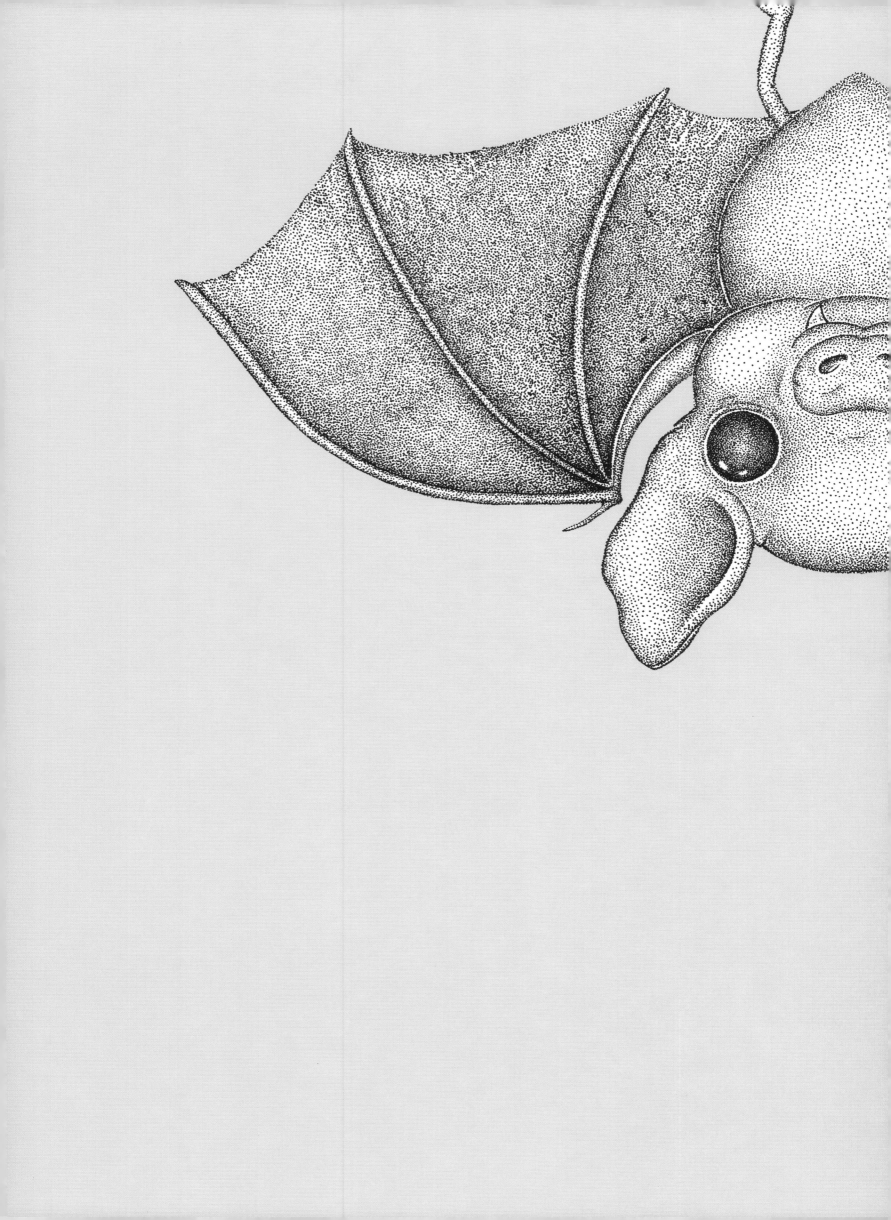

W

is for wombat

Walter the wombat is an Australian marsupial.
Female wombats have a pouch that faces
backwards, so they can dig without getting dirt in
their pouch, where a joey may be sleeping.

X

is for x-ray fish

Xavier the x-ray fish has a translucent layer of skin that covers his small body. This protects him from predators, as x-ray fish are quite hard to spot in shimmering water. A group of fish is called a 'school'.

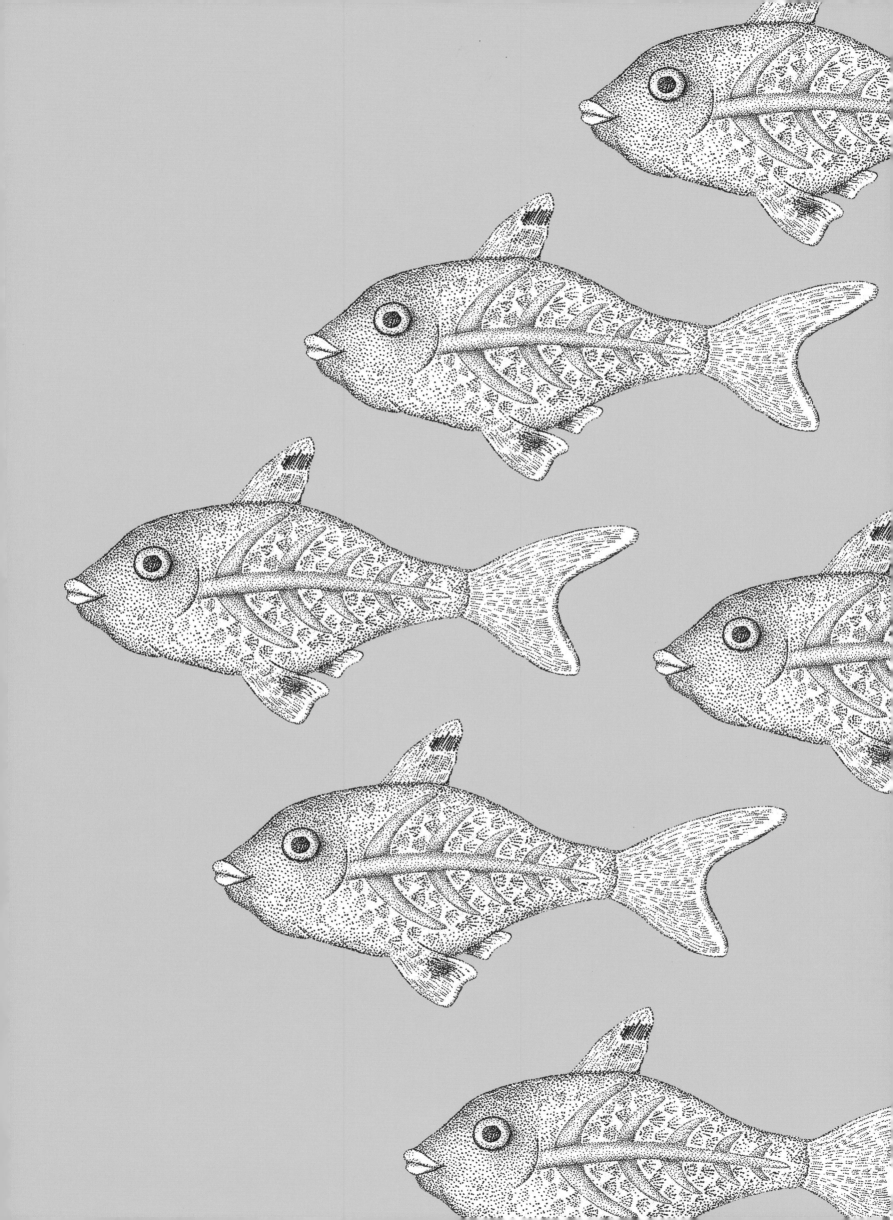

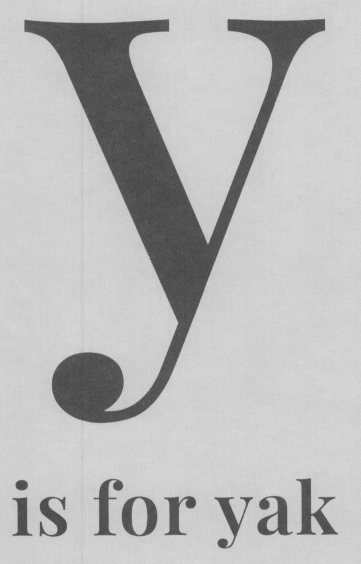

y

is for yak

Yanni the yak has a thick, warm coat that allows him to withstand very cold temperatures. Yaks like to live in herds, and they spend a lot of time grazing on grass and other plants.

Z

is for zebra

Zane the zebra is a close relative of the horse, native to Africa. Zebras are social animals that live in large herds. Each zebra's black-and-white striped coat has a unique pattern.

ABOUT THE ILLUSTRATOR

Donna Taylor is the Creative Illustrator behind Dots by Donna. Her unique dot artworks of people and animals are highly sought after all over the world, and have been exhibited in Australia, New York and Las Vegas. Donna is the recipient of numerous international awards, including NY NOW's Best New Product award.

Donna is self-taught and uses a freehand drawing technique known as 'stippling' or 'pointillism', using only a fineliner. Her illustrations are all original, with each piece taking 40–200 hours to complete.

Donna and her family live on the Sunshine Coast in Queensland, Australia.